Ladders

THE OLD WEST

GENRE Song

Read to find out about how the open range inspired poetry.

HOME ON THE RANGE

inspired by the poem "My Western Home" by Dr. Brewster Higley

In 1871, Dr. Brewster Higley left the eastern United States and moved to Kansas. He built a cabin on his own plot of land. The views surrounding the cabin inspired him to write a poem, and later the poem became a song. The original song was popular and many versions followed. Today we know the song by the title "Home on the Range." The lyrics below come from one of the most familiar versions of the song.

Oh, give me a home, where the buffalo roam
Where the deer and the **antelope** *play;*
Where seldom is heard a discouraging word,
And the skies are not cloudy all day.

(Refrain) Home, home on the **range**
Where the deer and the antelope play;
Where seldom is heard a discouraging word,
And the skies are not cloudy all day.

Where the air is so pure, the zephyrs so free,*
The breezes so balmy and light,
That I would not exchange my home on the range
For all the cities so bright.

(Refrain)

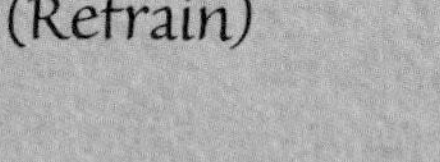

How often at night when the heavens are bright
With the light of the glittering stars,
Have I stood here amazed and asked as I gazed
If their glory exceeds that of ours.

(Refrain)

Oh, I love the wild flowers in this dear land of ours;
The curlew* I love to hear scream;
And I love the white rocks and the antelope flocks,
That graze on the mountain-tops green.

(Refrain)

Oh, give me a land where the bright diamond sand
Flows leisurely down the stream;
Where the graceful white swan goes gliding along
Like a maid in a heavenly dream.

(Refrain)

Then I would not exchange my home on the range,
Where the deer and the antelope play;
Where seldom is heard a discouraging word
And the skies are not cloudy all day.

(Refrain)

* curlew — a large shorebird with brown coloring that breeds in the Great Plains and has a long, curved bill

* zephyr — a gentle breeze that blows from the west

Check In How does the song convey details about the west?

GENRE Social Studies Article

Read to find out about the cowboys of the American Old West.

Cowboy History

by Dennis Fertig

Interstate highways stretch across the western United States. Every so often drivers will spy something in the dusty distance. “Can that be a cowboy?” they ask in surprise.

Well, yes it might be. Cowboys aren’t just legends of the past. Real cowboys still ride horses and patrol ranches to tend cattle—sometimes stubborn cattle. As they work, these cowboys see the modern highways in the distance, but they also see the long, proud tradition that they honor in their work. They follow the cowboy way that has lasted for centuries.

What was once considered "The West" included states west of the Mississippi River, Mexico, and part of western Canada.

What Is a Cowboy?

Throughout history, people have herded large groups of animals, such as sheep, goats, and pigs. A cowboy is a herder who cares for cattle. Animal herding might sound simple, but a cowboy's job has always been challenging and risky work.

The cowboy tradition started long before the United States existed. In the 1500s, Spanish soldiers and settlers brought two animals to North America: cattle and horses. Native Americans had never seen these large, strange-looking beasts before. Eventually though, many Native Americans became expert horsemen.

Cattle Ranching and *Vaqueros*

In Mexico and other areas where the Spanish settled, cattle ranching became common. Cattle are valuable animals. Cows provide milk that people drink and use to make cheese and butter. Cattle are also a source of meat, such as steak and hamburger meat. Leather is made from the hides of cattle. In the old days, soap and candles were made from cattle fat, and cattle dung was used as fuel.

Mexico had large, open areas for herds of cattle to roam, and wealthy Spaniards knew the land was perfect for ranching. *Vaqueros* were horsemen who worked for these ranchers. *Vaquero* means "cowman" in Spanish, and *vaqueros* were the first North American cowboys. They developed the handling techniques, clothing, and equipment that cowboys of the American West used. Some of the first cowboys were enslaved Native Americans forced to work on Spanish ranches.

Many English words about cowboy life come from Spanish words. For example, the word *buckaroo* was commonly used instead of cowboy. *Buckaroo* was how Americans who couldn't speak Spanish pronounced *vaquero.* The Spanish word for *wild* or *stray* was *mesteño.* Today we call wild horses mustangs.

Unique cowboy styles and names developed in different regions of the West.

The open **ranges** of the American West, particularly in Texas, became home to many mustangs. Cowboys caught wild horses. They broke them and the mustang became the cowboy's favorite horse to ride. As American settlers moved to Texas, some took up cattle ranching. New Texans, both ranchers and cowboys, learned how to handle horses from Mexican *vaqueros*.

Roundups and Cattle Drives

Until the Civil War started in 1861, cattle ranching thrived in Texas. The war slowed ranching. As a result the wild roaming herds of cattle grew larger. After the war, American **expansion** into the West began again. Cattle ranching restarted, making job opportunities for cowboys plentiful.

Ranchers were the land and cattle owners, but cowboys were the heart of cattle ranches. Ranchers relied heavily on the cowboys who lived and worked on the ranches. The cowboys were responsible for keeping cattle healthy and safe. They also protected the herd from rustlers, thieves who stole cattle.

There are many cattle breeds, but the most common in the Old West was the longhorn. Cowboys of the Old West became skilled in handling this breed. Longhorn cattle were a mixture of the breed the Spanish brought to America and an English breed from the eastern United States. Although longhorns were strong, stubborn, and had dangerous horns, these hard-to-handle animals also could travel long distances. They could live on small amounts of grass and water found in dry western lands.

Ranchers allowed their cattle to mix with other owners' cattle. Cattle had brands, or symbols, that cowboys burnt into cattle's hides with an iron tool. The brands showed which ranchers owned the cattle. Twice a year at roundups, cowboys herded cattle together and sorted them out by brand. Unbranded calves were claimed and then branded. Cattle could be rounded up and led to distant towns on train lines. The cattle were shipped by train. These long trips from ranges to railroads were called cattle drives. By 1867, cattle drives were becoming common. The great era of the cowboy had begun. About a third of the American cowboys were African American or Hispanic, and many cowboys had fought in the Civil War.

The Tools of the Cowboy

Almost everything a cowboy wore or carried was needed for his job.

Horse

The horse, a cowboy's most important tool, was trained to aid in rounding up longhorns. "Cutting horses" helped a cowboy capture and brand longhorns. Longhorns didn't want to be caught, so the horse and cowboy had to work together skillfully.

Clothing

Most cowboy clothing was similar to what Mexican cowboys wore.

Cowboys wore a scarf called a bandanna. Dipped in water and wrapped around his neck, a bandanna cooled a cowboy off. Worn around his face, it protected him from breathing trail dust. Most often, a bandanna just kept dust out of a cowboy's shirt.

Shirts, pants, and vests were usually made of a durable flannel material that absorbed sweat and didn't show dirt. Cowboys needed strong clothing to protect them from the weather and the rigors of their work.

Saddle

Cowboys often sat on saddles from sunrise to sundown, so a saddle had to be comfortable. The saddle's high back helped the cowboy stay put. Its front had a knob called a horn and was used to wrap a rope around. Hanging from the saddle were stirrups for a cowboy's feet. Under the stirrups were fenders, which kept the horse's sweat away from the cowboy.

Spurs

Cowboys wore spurs around the ankles of their boots. They poked spurs into the horse's side to get it to change direction. The spurs were dull but could get through thick horsehair.

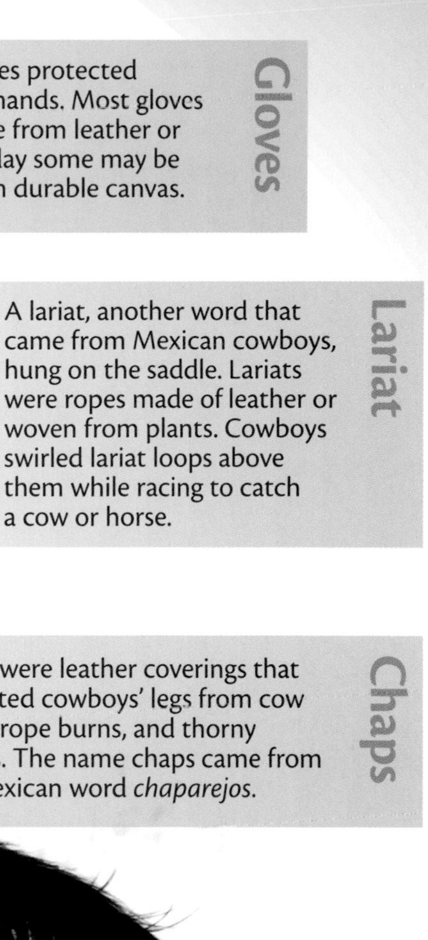

Gloves

Thick gloves protected cowboys' hands. Most gloves were made from leather or suede. Today some may be made from durable canvas.

Lariat

A lariat, another word that came from Mexican cowboys, hung on the saddle. Lariats were ropes made of leather or woven from plants. Cowboys swirled lariat loops above them while racing to catch a cow or horse.

Chaps

Chaps were leather coverings that protected cowboys' legs from cow horns, rope burns, and thorny bushes. The name chaps came from the Mexican word *chaparejos*.

Hat

A cowboy hat had a wide brim that protected the cowboy from sun, rain, and snow. It also protected his eyes and head from low branches. A cowboy could drink water from his hat or use it to feed his horse.

Boots

Boots were made of leather and designed so the heels and toes fit well into the stirrups of a saddle.

Cowboys, Dangers, and Guns

Trail life was dangerous. **Stampedes** could knock a cowboy off his horse; a longhorn could gore him; flash floods could drown him. Snakes, scorpions, or grizzlies could occasionally end his life suddenly and tragically.

Yet the dangers that make cowboy movies exciting were rare. Although battles with Native Americans were uncommon, cowboys did have guns, usually Colt pistols.

If a gun was shot, it was for a practical reason. Gunshots could be used as signals or to make stampeding cattle change direction.

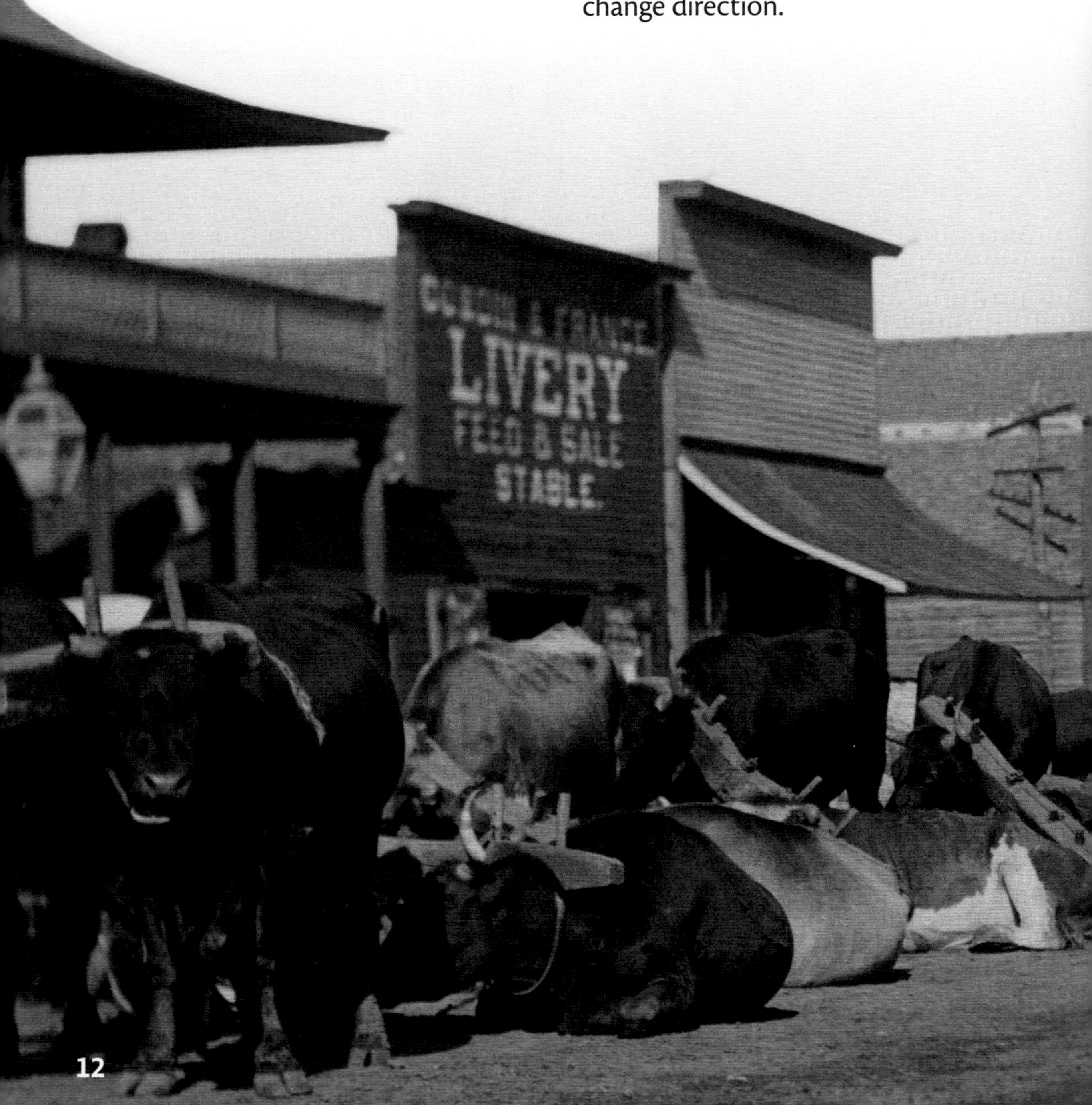

Cowboys shot plenty of threatening animals, but they didn't always wear guns. Pistols were heavy and got in the way of roping and riding, so cowboys often left their guns in the chuck wagon.

The End of the Trail

In the 1880s, expansion broadened and western territories filled with farmers and settlers. Barbed wire divided open ranges and turned them into closed ranches.

Longhorns were replaced with new cattle that didn't travel as well. But cattle didn't have to travel well because trains reached more places, and soon cattle drives were unnecessary.

The golden era of cowboys and cattle drives ended. It had lasted 30 years or so and involved about 30,000 real cowboys. But those hardy men made a lasting impression. Cowboy legends have lived ever since, and they always will.

Today tributes to The Old West are held annually in Sturgis, South Dakota. The photo below shows Sturgis's main street circa 1890.

Check In Why did the era of the cowboy on the trail come to an end?

GENRE **Historical Fiction** **Read to find out** about a legend of the American West.

ANNIE OAKLEY

POSTERS AROUND THE COUNTRY CALLED ANNIE A DEADEYE "**SHARPSHOOTER** FROM THE FAR WEST." SHE WAS AN INCREDIBLY GOOD SHOT, BUT SHE GUARDED A DEEP SECRET.

FRANK WAS CELEBRATED AS A SKILLED ***MARKSMAN.*** YET ON A FATEFUL DAY, A SHOCKING SHOOTING CONTEST LED HIM TO LAY DOWN HIS GUNS FOREVER.

AND THE WILD WEST SHOW

BY DENNIS FERTIG · ILLUSTRATED BY FEDERICO PIATTI

CAPTAIN ADAM H. BOGARDUS

THIS WILY OLD CAPTAIN WAS THE WILD WEST SHOW'S TOP MARKSMAN. NO ONE THOUGHT HE WOULD EVER LEAVE THE SHOW, THAT IS, UNTIL TRAGEDY STRUCK.

BUFFALO BILL CODY

WILLIAM CODY PRODUCED A SHOW THAT DEPICTED LEGENDARY MOMENTS OF THE REAL AMERICAN WEST. THE SHOW WAS **AUTHENTIC**—EXCEPT FOR THE MOST SUCCESSFUL PART.

NATE SALSBURY

THIS MYSTERY MAN WHO OPERATED IN THE SHADOWS HAD A LASTING EFFECT ON THE WILD WEST. WAS ALL THAT POWER A GOOD THING?

PHOEBE ANN MOSES WAS BORN IN 1860, THE FIFTH DAUGHTER IN A DARKE COUNTY, OHIO, PIONEER FAMILY. AS THEY WORKED THEIR SMALL FARM, THE MOSES FAMILY HAD BOTH FRUITFUL YEARS AND CHALLENGING ONES.
PHOEBE IS TOO FANCY OF A NAME FOR OUR SISTER.
LET'S JUST CALL THE BABY *ANNIE*.

ANNIE'S MOTHER AND SISTERS LABORED DAILY DOING THE DIFFICULT THINGS THAT PIONEER WOMEN ALWAYS DID.
WE'LL HAVE PLENTY OF BEETS FOR NOW AND FOR CANNING FOR WINTER.
IT IS SO, SO HARD DIGGING THE BEETS OUT OF THE HARD GROUND!

YOUNG ANNIE WORKED HARD AS WELL, BUT PREFERRED TO TRAP AND HUNT, LIKE THE PIONEER MEN.
LET'S HOPE THIS CORNSTALK TRAP WILL CATCH US A BIG, FAT BIRD.
A TURKEY DINNER WOULD BE SO MUCH BETTER THAN BEETS!

ANNIE WASN'T ALLOWED TO SHOOT LIKE THE MEN WERE, BUT THERE WAS A RUMOR THAT SHE BORROWED HER FATHER'S RIFLE WHEN SHE WAS JUST EIGHT YEARS OLD.
I JUST HOPE THAT WILD TURKEY DOESN'T DECIDE TO MOVE.

SHARP-EYED TEENAGER ANNIE HUNTED SMALL GAME—WILD TURKEY, QUAIL, AND RABBIT—AND SOLD THEM TO A LOCAL STORE. FROM THOSE DAYS UNTIL SHE DIED MANY DECADES LATER, ANNIE EARNED HER LIVING WITH HER SHOOTING SKILLS.
WHERE DID THAT LITTLE GIRL GET SUCH A BASKETFUL OF FRESH GAME?
OPEN
THAT LITTLE GIRL IS ANNIE MOSES, THE BEST SHOT IN DARKE COUNTY—AND MAYBE THE WHOLE WORLD.

THIS YOUNG WOMAN MAY BE WORTH WATCHING.

IN THOSE DAYS, PEOPLE LOVED SHARPSHOOTING. SKILL WITH A RIFLE OR SHOTGUN WAS OFTEN NECESSARY IN AMERICA'S WILDER TERRITORIES, AND IT WAS ADMIRED EVERYWHERE. CONTESTS AT SHOOTING **RANGES** DREW FAMOUS SHOOTERS AND LARGE AUDIENCES.

AMERICA'S BEST-KNOWN MARKSMEN WERE CAPTAIN ADAM H. BOGARDUS AND DOC CARVER. FRANK BUTLER WAS ALMOST AS FAMOUS AND ALMOST AS GOOD, OR SO HE THOUGHT.

WHEN FRANK BUTLER ACCEPTED THE WAGER, HE ASSUMED THAT THE CHAMPION WOULD BE A MAN WHO COULD EASILY BE BEATEN. WHEN HE DISCOVERED THAT THE COUNTY CHAMP WAS A YOUNG WOMAN, ANNIE MOSES, FRANK WAS STUNNED.

FRANK BUTLER'S AMAZEMENT GREW WHEN HE LOST THE SHOOTING MATCH.

CRASH

CRASH

AS IMPRESSED AS FRANK WAS BY ANNIE'S SHOOTING, HE WAS EVEN MORE IMPRESSED BY HER PERSONALITY. FRANK FELL IN LOVE WITH THE YOUNG MARKSWOMAN. ANNIE SOON FELL IN LOVE WITH FRANK, AND THEY MARRIED IN 1876.

ANNIE OAKLEY
SHARPSHOOTER FROM THE FAR WEST
SELLS BROTHERS
CIRCUS & MENAGERIE
ANNIE USED THE STAGE NAME *ANNIE OAKLEY,* AND SHE AND FRANK STARTED A SHOOTING ACT TOGETHER CALLED "BUTLER & OAKLEY." IN THE SELLS BROTHERS CIRCUS, ANNIE WAS CALLED A "SHARPSHOOTER FROM THE FAR WEST."
MY SECRET IS THAT I NEVER LIVED IN THE WEST.
THE CROWDS WILL ALWAYS CHEER FOR YOU, ANNIE, NO MATTER WHERE YOU ARE FROM!
ANNIE AND FRANK HOPED TO JOIN BUFFALO BILL'S WILD WEST SHOW WHERE THEY KNEW ANNIE WOULD BE A REAL SHOOTING STAR. THEY HOPED THEY COULD GET BUFFALO BILL INTERESTED IN HER.
"DEAR MR. CODY,
I WRITE TODAY TO INFORM YOU ABOUT A REMARKABLY TALENTED YOUNG MARKSWOMAN . . ."

BUFFALO BILL CODY WAS BORN IN 1846 AND BECAME AN AUTHENTIC WESTERN HERO. DURING HIS LIFETIME, HE WAS A PONY EXPRESS RIDER,

. . . A UNION SOLDIER,

. . . A BUFFALO HUNTER,

. . . AND A SCOUT FOR THE U.S. CAVALRY.
HE BATTLED AND LATER BEFRIENDED NATIVE AMERICANS.

IN THE 1880S, THE AMERICAN WEST BEGAN TO CHANGE. BUFFALO BILL DECIDED TO COMMEMORATE ITS SPIRIT WITH HIS WILD WEST SHOW. MILLIONS OF PEOPLE WATCHED AS BUFFALO BILL'S TROUPE CELEBRATED THE EXCITING DAYS OF ADVENTURE IN THE OLD WEST.

BUFFALO BILL'S WILD WEST SHOW DELIGHTED PEOPLE WORLDWIDE FOR 30 YEARS.
BUFFALO BILL STUDIED FRANK'S LETTER, CONSIDERED HIS REQUEST, AND REJECTED IT. THE WILD WEST SHOW ALREADY HAD AMERICA'S TOP SHARPSHOOTING ACT FEATURING CAPTAIN BOGARDUS AND HIS FOUR SONS. PLUS, BUFFALO BILL WORRIED THAT ANNIE WAS TOO FRAGILE TO HANDLE SHOTGUNS EVERY DAY.
"DEAR MR. BUTLER,
I AM IMPRESSED BY ANNIE OAKLEY'S GREAT SKILL BUT REGRET . . ."

YET WITHIN WEEKS, TRAGEDY STRUCK AND THINGS CHANGED. THE WILD WEST SHOW'S STEAMBOAT COLLIDED WITH ANOTHER BOAT AND SUNK IN THE MISSISSIPPI RIVER. MUCH OF THE SHOW'S EQUIPMENT, INCLUDING CAPTAIN BOGARDUS'S GUNS, SUNK INTO THE MURKY WATERS.
NO GUNS AND NO EQUIPMENT MEANS I QUIT!
BUFFALO BILL NEEDED A NEW SHARPSHOOTER ACT, SO HE RELUCTANTLY INVITED ANNIE TO LOUISVILLE FOR AN AUDITION.
I STILL DON'T KNOW IF SUCH A SMALL PERSON CAN HANDLE THOSE HEAVY SHOTGUNS.
THIS YOUNG ANNIE OAKLEY IS MUCH STRONGER THAN SHE LOOKS.
ANNIE AND FRANK TOOK A TRAIN TO CINCINNATI WHERE THEY COULD PRACTICE FOR SEVERAL WEEKS ON A FANCY TRAPSHOOTING RANGE.
213

TO PROVE THAT SHE WAS READY FOR THE WILD WEST SHOW AND WASN'T TOO FRAGILE TO HANDLE HEAVY SHOTGUNS, FRANK GAVE ANNIE A TOUGH TEST. FRANK USED THEIR SMALL TRAPSHOOTING MACHINES TO FLING GLASS BALLS HIGH INTO THE AIR. IN ONE DAY, FRANK SENT 5,000 BALLS SKYWARD, AND ANNIE HIT 4,772 OF THEM.
NO ONE CAN OUTSHOOT THIS DAZZLING YOUNG SHARPSHOOTER!
AND FEW MEN CAN HANDLE A HEAVY SHOTGUN LIKE THAT SMALL, YOUNG WOMAN DOES.
BLAM
BLAM
CRASH
CRASH
UNBELIEVABLE! NEARLY ALL 5,000 HIT!
ANNIE'S TARGETS WERE GLASS BALLS FILLED WITH FEATHERS.
CRASH

WHEN THE BIG DAY IN LOUISVILLE FINALLY ARRIVED, ANNIE PRACTICED HER ACT ONCE MORE IN AN EMPTY BASEBALL PARK. FRANK SET UP TARGETS AND FLUNG BALLS INTO THE AIR, WHILE MYSTERY MAN NATE SALSBURY SECRETLY OBSERVED.

ANNIE STOOD ON ONE SIDE OF A TABLE AND WAITED FOR A BALL TO SPIRAL INTO THE AIR.

THEN ANNIE LEAPED OVER THE TABLE,

. . . GRABBED A SHOTGUN,

. . . AND FIRED, EXPLODING THE TARGET IN MID-AIR.

NATE SALSBURY, A WILD WEST SHOW TALENT SCOUT AND BUFFALO BILL'S BUSINESS PARTNER, WAS THE SPY IN ANNIE'S LIFE. THAT MORNING, NATE HIRED ANNIE AND FRANK ON THE SPOT WITHOUT CHECKING WITH BUFFALO BILL.

ANNIE OAKLEY

BUFFALO BILL'S WILD WEST

ANNIE QUICKLY BECAME THE BIGGEST SUCCESS IN THE WILD WEST SHOW, EVEN THOUGH SHE HAD NEVER LIVED IN THE WEST!

Check In Why did Bill Cody change his mind about Annie Oakley?

Discuss Information

1. How do you think the three pieces in this book relate to the theme of *The Old West*?

2. How does the speaker's point of view affect the description of the setting in the song "Home on the Range"?

3. What information from "Cowboy History" was most interesting to you? Why?

4. Look at pp. 8 and 9 in "Cowboy History." What items protected cowboys from weather and other natural elements? How do they do that?

5. "Annie Oakley and the Wild West Show" is historical fiction that is based on real life. Look at the illustrations of clothing and gear. How are they similar to the authentic cowboy gear shown in "Cowboy History"?

6. What do you still want to learn about The Old West? What questions do you have about the time period and the people?